Am I a Bully?

" Being bullied is a very painful experience and has caused many children to harm themselves due to that pain.This book is intended to get kids, parents and teachers talking about bullying and gaining a better understanding of what it looks like to be a bully and how to address it."

Hope Gilchrist 2018

My name is Toby and I am 11 years old. I have a big brother and two little sisters and we live with our mom and dad. I also have three very good friends that I hang out with at school.

Felix, Stan and Bre' are my best friends. We like to play around and joke a lot. We like to hang out in front of the school before school begins. I am popular at school. It seems like everyone knows my name which excites me.

We have fun in our all our classes but we have the most fun in Mrs. Casey's class. We sometimes goof around in class when we should be learning.

We laugh at the funny things we see. We laugh a lot at Parker because he always wears these funny looking shoes and that gross blue sweater.

Parker doesn't dress like the rest of us. Sometimes I yell his name and tell him I like his ugly blue sweater but I really don't. It makes my friends laugh.

Parker doesn't say much when we laugh at him he just sits there. One day he did ask us to stop but we were just joking. Felix says I am being too hard on Parker. I am just being funny; I am not being mean.

Yesterday, Parker wore those brown shoes that no one else wears and boy that was funny. Mrs. Casey said that it wasn't nice so I stopped but my friends kept laughing in a lower voice.

Bullies beat people up, knock their books down and take their lunch money. I don't do that. My sisters and brother laugh at me at home. Laughing is normal it's just what people do.

Some of the other kids in my class say I am being a bully but I don't think I am. I am just being funny. I have never hit or pushed Parker.

Parker looks at us with a mean face but he doesn't say anything. I tell him to ease up. I let him know that we are just joking and suggest he wear something else.

The other kids on the bus laugh when I tell him to wear something else. When Parker gets off the bus he doesn't look that mad. The bus driver tells me she thinks I am mean and being a bully to Parker and I need to stop.

I was a little angry when I came home because Ms. Cathy, the bus driver, was mean to me. She doesn't even know me. I am just a funny person. Bullies are big and scary and I am not scary. I am Toby the funny sunny bunny "Ha, Ha, Ha."

I watch television while I do my homework. Dinner is after homework. My family always laughs a lo
during dinner time.

During dinner, I asked my mom if I was a bully. She looked at me with a confused face and replied "I don't think so."

My mom asked me where that question came from and wanted to know who had called me a bully. I told mom some kids in my school and my bus driver said I was a bully because I like to make jokes.

Mom asked if my jokes are putting people down and do I hurt their feelings. I told her I am not trying to hurt anyone's feelings I just like making my friends laugh.

My sister said if the other person doesn't think it is funny and is not laughing along then I may be being a bully. I told them I am not a bully because I am not beating anyone up or taking their lunch money

Mom says you don't have to hit or punch or take someone's lunch money to be called a bully. Mom explains to me that I can be a bully if I tease someone a lot and laugh at them when they don't think it's funny. Bullying also happens when you put someone down in front of other people.

Mom told me that if making everyone else laugh hurts someone else's feelings then I am being a bully. She said she hopes that's not what I am doing at school.

Mom says she wants me to apologize to Parker for bullying him. I will apologize because I didn't know I was being a bully and being a bully is wrong.

Tomorrow I must tell my friends what I learned about bullying, "Now, off to dream land I go."

Made in the USA
Middletown, DE
19 August 2020

15992642R00015